RED BIRD

OTHER BOOKS BY MARY OLIVER

POETRY
No Voyage and Other Poems
The River Styx, Ohio, and Other Poems
Twelve Moons
American Primitive
Dream Work
House of Light
New and Selected Poems Volume One
White Pine
West Wind
The Leaf and the Cloud
What Do We Know
Owls and Other Fantasies
Why I Wake Early
Blue Iris
New and Selected Poems Volume Two
Thirst

CHAPBOOKS AND SPECIAL EDITIONS
The Night Traveler
Sleeping in the Forest
Provincetown
Wild Geese (UK Edition)

PROSE
A Poetry Handbook
Blue Pastures
Rules for the Dance
Winter Hours
Long Life
Our World (with photographs by Molly Malone Cook)

RED BIRD

Poems by

Mary Oliver

BEACON PRESS

BOSTON

Beacon Press
25 Beacon Street
Boston, Massachusetts 02108-2892
www.beacon.org

Beacon Press books
are published under the auspices of
the Unitarian Universalist Association of Congregations.

24   14

This book is printed on acid-free paper that meets the
uncoated paper ANSI/NISO specifications for permanence
as revised in 1992.

Library of Congress Cataloging-in-Publication Data

Oliver, Mary
Red bird : poems / by Mary Oliver.
p. cm.
ISBN-13: 978-0-8070-6893-9
I. Title.
PS3565.L5R43 2008
811'.54—dc22
2007035357

CONTENTS

But I always think that the best way
to know God is to love many things.
—Vincent van Gogh

RED BIRD

Red Bird

Red bird came all winter
firing up the landscape
as nothing else could.

Of course I love the sparrows,
those dun-colored darlings,
so hungry and so many.

I am a God-fearing feeder of birds.
I know He has many children,
not all of them bold in spirit.

Still, for whatever reason—
perhaps because the winter is so long
and the sky so black-blue,

or perhaps because the heart narrows
as often as it opens—
I am grateful

that red bird comes all winter
firing up the landscape
as nothing else can do.

Luke

I had a dog
  who loved flowers.
    Briskly she went
      through the fields,

yet paused
  for the honeysuckle
    or the rose,
      her dark head

and her wet nose
  touching
    the face
      of every one

with its petals
  of silk,
    with its fragrance
      rising

into the air
  where the bees,
    their bodies
      heavy with pollen,

hovered—
  and easily
    she adored
      every blossom,

not in the serious,
  careful way
    that we choose
      this blossom or that blossom—

the way we praise or don't praise—
  the way we love
    or don't love—
      but the way

we long to be—
  that happy
    in the heaven of earth—
      that wild, that loving.

Maker of All Things, Even Healings

All night
under the pines
the fox
moves through the darkness
with a mouthful of teeth
and a reputation for death
which it deserves.
In the spicy
villages of the mice
he is famous,
his nose
in the grass
is like an earthquake,
his feet
on the path
is a message so absolute
that the mouse, hearing it,
makes himself
as small as he can
as he sits silent
or, trembling, goes on
hunting among the grasses
for the ripe seeds.
Maker of All Things,
including appetite,
including stealth,
including the fear that makes
all of us, sometime or other,

flee for the sake
of our small and precious lives,
let me abide in your shadow—
let me hold on
to the edge of your robe
as you determine
what you must let be lost
and what will be saved.

There Is a Place Beyond Ambition

When the flute players
couldn't think of what to say next

they laid down their pipes,
then they lay down themselves
beside the river

and just listened.
Some of them, after a while,
jumped up
and disappeared back inside the busy town.
But the rest—
so quiet, not even thoughtful—
are still there,

still listening.

Self-Portrait

I wish I was twenty and in love with life
   and still full of beans.

Onward, old legs!
There are the long, pale dunes; on the other side
the roses are blooming and finding their labor
no adversity to the spirit.

Upward, old legs! There are the roses, and there is the sea
shining like a song, like a body
I want to touch

though I'm not twenty
and won't be again but ah! seventy. And still
in love with life. And still
full of beans.

Night and the River

I have seen the great feet
leaping
into the river

and I have seen moonlight
milky
along the long muzzle

and I have seen the body
of something
scaled and wonderful

slumped in the sudden fire of its mouth,
and I could not tell
which fit me

more comfortably, the power,
or the powerlessness;
neither would have me

entirely; I was divided,
consumed,
by sympathy,

pity, admiration.
After a while
it was done,

the fish had vanished, the bear
lumped away
to the green shore

and into the trees. And then there was only
this story.
It followed me home

and entered my house—
a difficult guest
with a single tune

which it hums all day and through the night—
slowly or briskly,
it doesn't matter,

it sounds like a river leaping and falling;
it sounds like a body
falling apart.

Boundaries

There is a place where the town ends,
    and the fields begin.
It's not marked but the feet know it,
also the heart that is longing for refreshment
    and, equally, for repose.

Someday we'll live in the sky.
Meanwhile, the house of our lives is this green world.
The fields, the ponds, the birds.
The thick black oaks—surely they are
    the invention of something wonderful.
And the tiger lilies.
And the runaway honeysuckle that no one
    will ever trim again.

Where is it? I ask, and then
my feet know it.

One jump, and I'm home.

Straight Talk from Fox

Listen says fox it is music to run
  over the hills to lick
dew from the leaves to nose along
  the edges of the ponds to smell the fat
ducks in their bright feathers but
  far out, safe in their rafts of
sleep. It is like
  music to visit the orchard, to find
the vole sucking the sweet of the apple, or the
  rabbit with his fast-beating heart. Death itself
is a music. Nobody has ever come close to
  writing it down, awake or in a dream. It cannot
be told. It is flesh and bones
  changing shape and with good cause, mercy
is a little child beside such an invention. It is
  music to wander the black back roads
outside of town no one awake or wondering
  if anything miraculous is ever going to
happen, totally dumb to the fact of every
  moment's miracle. Don't think I haven't
peeked into windows. I see you in all your seasons
  making love, arguing, talking about God
as if he were an idea instead of the grass,
  instead of the stars, the rabbit caught
in one good teeth-whacking hit and brought
  home to the den. What I am, and I know it, is
responsible, joyful, thankful. I would not
  give my life for a thousand of yours.

Another Everyday Poem

Every day
  I consider
    the lilies—
      how they are dressed—

and the ravens—
  how they are fed—
    and how each of these
      is a miracle

of Lord-love
  and of sorrow—
    for the lilies
      in their bright dresses

cannot last
  but wrinkle fast
    and fall,
      and the little ravens

in their windy nest
  rise up
    in such pleasure
      at the sight

of fresh meat
  that makes their lives sweet—
    and what a puzzle it is
      that such brevity—

the lavish clothes,
the ruddy food—
makes the world
so full, so good.

Visiting the Graveyard

When I think of death
it is a bright enough city,
and every year more faces there
are familiar

but not a single one
notices me,
though I long for it,
and when they talk together,

which they do
very quietly,
it's in an unknowable language—
I can catch the tone

but understand not a single word—
and when I open my eyes
there's the mysterious field, the beautiful trees.
There are the stones.

Ocean

I am in love with Ocean
lifting her thousands of white hats
in the chop of the storm,
or lying smooth and blue, the
loveliest bed in the world.
In the personal life, there is

always grief more than enough,
a heart-load for each one of us
on the dusty road. I suppose
there is a reason for this, so I will be
patient, acquiescent. But I will live
nowhere except here, by Ocean, trusting
equally in all the blast and welcome
of her sorrowless, salt self.

With the Blackest of Inks

At night
  the panther,
    who is lean
      and quick,

is only
  a pair of eyes
    and, with a yawn,
      momentarily,

a long, pink tongue.
  Mostly
    he listens
      as he walks

on the puffs
  of his feet
    as if
      on a carpet

from Persia,
  or leaps
    into the branches
      of a tree,

or swims
  across the river,
    or simply
      stands in the grass

and waits.
   Because, Sir,
      you have given him,
         for your own reasons,

everything that he needs:
   leaves, food, shelter;
      a conscience
         that never blinks.

Invitation

Oh do you have time
  to linger
    for just a little while
     out of your busy

and very important day
  for the goldfinches
    that have gathered
     in a field of thistles

for a musical battle,
  to see who can sing
    the highest note,
     or the lowest,

or the most expressive of mirth,
  or the most tender?
    Their strong, blunt beaks
     drink the air

as they strive
  melodiously
    not for your sake
     and not for mine

and not for the sake of winning
  but for sheer delight and gratitude—
    believe us, they say,
     it is a serious thing

just to be alive
   on this fresh morning
      in this broken world.
         I beg of you,

do not walk by
   without pausing
      to attend to this
         rather ridiculous performance.

It could mean something.
   It could mean everything.
      It could be what Rilke meant, when he wrote:
         You must change your life.

The Orchard

I have dreamed
of accomplishment.
I have fed

ambition.
I have traded
nights of sleep

for a length of work.
Lo, and I have discovered
how soft bloom

turns to green fruit
which turns to sweet fruit.
Lo, and I have discovered

all winds blow cold
at last,
and the leaves,

so pretty, so many,
vanish
in the great, black

packet of time,
in the great, black
packet of ambition,

and the ripeness
of the apple
is its downfall.

A River Far Away and Long Ago

The river
  of my childhood,
    that tumbled
      down a passage of rocks

and cut-work ferns,
  came here and there
    to the swirl
      and slowdown

of a pool
  and I saw myself—
    oh, clearly—
      as I knelt at one—

then I saw myself
  as if carried away,
    as the river moved on.
      Where have I gone?

Since then
  I have looked and looked
    for myself,
      not sure

who I am, or where,
  or, more importantly, why.
    It's okay—
      I have had a wonderful life.

Still, I ponder
　　where that other is—
　　　　where I landed,
　　　　　　what I thought, what I did,

what small or even maybe meaningful deeds
　　I might have accomplished
　　　　somewhere
　　　　　　among strangers,

coming to them
　　as only a river can—
　　　　touching every life it meets—
　　　　　　that endlessly kind, that enduring.

Night Herns

Some herons
were fishing
in the robes
of the night

at a low hour
of the water's body,
and the fish, I suppose,
were full

of fish happiness
in those transparent inches
even as, over and over,
the beaks jacked down

and the narrow
bodies were lifted
with every
quick sally,

and that was the end of them
as far as we know—
though, what do we know
except that death

is so everywhere and so entire—
pummeling and felling,
or sometimes,
like this, appearing

through such a thin door—
one stab, and you're through!
And what then?
Why, then it was almost morning,

and one by one
the birds
opened their wings
and flew.

Summer Story

When the hummingbird
sinks its face
into the trumpet vine,
into the funnels

of the blossoms,
and the tongue
leaps out
and throbs,

I am scorched
to realize once again
how many small, available things
are in this world

that aren't
pieces of gold
or power—
that nobody owns

or could buy even
for a hillside of money—
that just
float about the world,

or drift over the fields,
or into the gardens,
and into the tents of the vines,
and now here I am

spending my time,
as the saying goes,
watching until the watching turns into feeling,
so that I feel I am myself

a small bird
with a terrible hunger,
with a thin beak probing and dipping
and a heart that races so fast

it is only a heartbeat ahead of breaking—
and I am the hunger and the assuagement,
and also I am the leaves and the blossoms,
and, like them, I am full of delight, and shaking.

The Teachers

Owl in the black morning,
  mockingbird in the burning
    slants of the sunny afternoon
      declare so simply

to the world
  everything I have tried but still
    haven't been able
      to put into words,

so I do not go
  far from that school
    with its star-bright
      or blue ceiling,

and I listen to those teachers,
  and others too—
    the wind in the trees
      and the water waves—

for they are what lead me
  from the dryness of self
    where I labor
      with the mind-steps of language—

lonely, as we all are
  in the singular,
    I listen hard
      to the exuberances

of the mockingbird and the owl,
   the waves and the wind.
      And then, like peace after perfect speech,
      such stillness.

Percy and Books (Eight)

Percy does not like it when I read a book.
He puts his face over the top of it and moans.
He rolls his eyes, sometimes he sneezes.
The sun is up, he says, and the wind is down.
The tide is out and the neighbor's dogs are playing.
But Percy, I say. Ideas! The elegance of language!
The insights, the funniness, the beautiful stories
that rise and fall and turn into strength, or courage.

Books? says Percy. I ate one once, and it was enough.
Let's go.

Summer Morning

Heart,
  I implore you,
    it's time to come back
    from the dark,

it's morning,
  the hills are pink
    and the roses
      whatever they felt

in the valley of night
  are opening now
    their soft dresses,
      their leaves

are shining.
  Why are you laggard?
    Sure you have seen this
      a thousand times,

which isn't half enough.
  Let the world
    have its way with you,
      luminous as it is

with mystery
  and pain—
    graced as it is
      with the ordinary.

Small Bodies

It is almost summer. In the pond
the pickerel leap,
and the delicate teal have brought forth
their many charming young,
and the turtle is ravenous.
It is hard sometimes, oh Lord,
to be faithful.
I am more boldly made
than the little ducks, paddling and laughing.
But not so bold
as the turtle
with his greasy mouth.
I know you know everything—
I rely on this.
Still, there are so many small bodies in the world,
for which I am afraid.

Winter and the Nuthatch

Once or twice and maybe again, who knows,
the timid nuthatch will come to me
if I stand still, with something good to eat in my hand.
The first time he did it
he landed smack on his belly, as though
the legs wouldn't cooperate. The next time
he was bolder. Then he became absolutely
wild about those walnuts.

But there was a morning I came late and, guess what,
the nuthatch was flying into a stranger's hand.
To speak plainly, I felt betrayed.
I wanted to say: Mister,
that nuthatch and I have a relationship.
It took hours of standing in the snow
before he would drop from the tree and trust my fingers.
But I didn't say anything.

Nobody owns the sky or the trees.
Nobody owns the hearts of birds.
Still, being human and partial therefore to my own
    successes—
though not resentful of others fashioning theirs—

I'll come tomorrow, I believe, quite early.

Crow Says

There is corn in the field,
what should I think of else?

Anyway, my thoughts are all feathery.
I prefer simple beak talk.

Maybe it's having wings.
It does make a difference.

As for that business about brothers,
of course I'm concerned that we

share the corn, to the extent
that I get my plenty.

As for later, how can "later" exist?
When old crows die I don't cry,

I peck at their silly, staring eyes
and open my wings and fly to

wherever I want to. I've forgotten
both father and mother,

even the pile of sticks
in which I was born. Well, maybe

now and again, and mostly in winter,
I have strange, even painful ruminations.

When you're hungry and cold
it's hard to be bold, so I sulk,

and I do have dreams sometimes, in which
I remember the corn will come again,

and vaguely then I feel that I am almost feeling
grateful, to something or other.

Sometimes

1.

Something came up
out of the dark.
It wasn't anything I had ever seen before.
It wasn't an animal
   or a flower,
unless it was both.

Something came up out of the water,
   a head the size of a cat
but muddy and without ears.
I don't know what God is.
I don't know what death is.

But I believe they have between them
   some fervent and necessary arrangement.

2.

Sometimes
melancholy leaves me breathless.

3.

Later I was in a field full of sunflowers.
I was feeling the heat of midsummer.
I was thinking of the sweet, electric
   drowse of creation,

when it began to break.

In the west, clouds gathered.
Thunderheads.
In an hour the sky was filled with them.

In an hour the sky was filled
   with the sweetness of rain and the blast of lightning.
Followed by the deep bells of thunder.

Water from the heavens! Electricity from the source!
Both of them mad to create something!

The lightning brighter than any flower.
The thunder without a drowsy bone in its body.

4.

Instructions for living a life:
Pay attention.
Be astonished.
Tell about it.

5.

Two or three times in my life I discovered love.
Each time it seemed to solve everything.
Each time it solved a great many things
    but not everything.
Yet left me as grateful as if it had indeed, and
  thoroughly, solved everything.

6.

God, rest in my heart
and fortify me,
take away my hunger for answers,
let the hours play upon my body

like the hands of my beloved.
Let the cathead appear again—
the smallest of your mysteries,
some wild cousin of my own blood probably—
some cousin of my own wild blood probably,
in the black dinner-bowl of the pond.

7.

Death waits for me, I know it, around
    one corner or another.
This doesn't amuse me.
Neither does it frighten me.

After the rain, I went back into the field of sunflowers.
It was cool, and I was anything but drowsy.
I walked slowly, and listened

to the crazy roots, in the drenched earth, laughing and growing.

Percy (Nine)

Your friend is coming I say
to Percy, and name a name

and he runs to the door, his
wide mouth in its laugh-shape,

and waves, since he has one, his tail.
Emerson, I am trying to live,

as you said we must, the examined life.
But there are days I wish

there was less in my head to examine,
not to speak of the busy heart. How

would it be to be Percy, I wonder, not
thinking, not weighing anything, just running forward.

Black Swallowtail

The caterpillar,
    interesting but not exactly lovely,
humped along among the parsley leaves
    eating, always eating. Then
one night it was gone and in its place
    a small green confinement hung by two silk threads
on a parsley stem. I think it took nothing with it
    except faith, and patience. And then one morning

it expressed itself into the most beautiful being.

Red

All the while
I was teaching
in the state of Virginia
I wanted to see
gray fox.
Finally I found him.
He was in the highway.
He was singing
his death song.
I picked him up
and carried him
into a field
while the cars kept coming.
He showed me
how he could ripple
how he could bleed.
Goodbye I said
to the light of his eye
as the cars went by.
Two mornings later
I found the other.
She was in the highway.
She was singing
her death song.
I picked her up

and carried her
into the field
where she rippled
half of her gray
half of her red
while the cars kept coming.
While the cars kept coming.
Gray fox and gray fox.
Red, red, red.

Showing the Birds

Look, children, here is the shy,
flightless dodo; the many-colored
pigeon named the passenger, the
great auk, the Eskimo curlew, the
woodpecker called the Lord God Bird,
the . . .
Come, children, hurry—there are so many
more wonderful things to show you in
the museum's dark drawers.

From This River, When I Was a Child, I Used to Drink

But when I came back I found
that the body of the river was dying.

"Did it speak?"

Yes, it sang out the old songs, but faintly.

"What will you do?"

I will grieve of course, but that's nothing.

"What, precisely, will you grieve for?"

For the river. For myself, my lost
joyfulness. For the children who will not
know what a river can be—a friend, a
companion, a hint of heaven.

"Isn't this somewhat overplayed?"

I said: it can be a friend. A companion. A
hint of heaven.

Watching a Documentary about Polar Bears
Trying to Survive on the Melting Ice Floes

That God had a plan, I do not doubt.
But what if His plan was, that we would do better?

Of The Empire

We will be known as a culture that feared death
and adored power, that tried to vanquish insecurity
for the few and cared little for the penury of the
many. We will be known as a culture that taught
and rewarded the amassing of things, that spoke
little if at all about the quality of life for
people (other people), for dogs, for rivers. All
the world, in our eyes, they will say, was a
commodity. And they will say that this structure
was held together politically, which it was, and
they will say also that our politics was no more
than an apparatus to accommodate the feelings of
the heart, and that the heart, in those days,
was small, and hard, and full of meanness.

Not This, Not That

Nor anything,
not the eastern wind whose other name
   is rain,
nor the burning heats of the dunes
    at the crown of summer,
nor the ticks, that new, ferocious populace,

not the President who loves blood,
nor the governmental agencies that love money,

will alter

my love for you, my friends and my beloved,
or for you, oh ghosts of Emerson and Whitman,

or for you, oh blue sky of a summer morning,
that makes me roll in a barrel of gratitude
   down hills,

or for you, oldest of friends: hope;
or for you, newest of friends: faith;

or for you, silliest and dearest of surprises, my
own life.

Iraq

I want to sing a song
   for a body I saw
      crumpled
         and without a name

but clearly someone young
   who had not yet lived his life
      and never would.
         How shall I do this?

What kind of song
   would serve such a purpose?
      This poem may never end,
         for what answer does it have

for anyone
   in this distant,
      comfortable country,
         simply looking on?

Clearly
   he had a weapon in his hands.
      I think
         he could have been no more than twenty.

I think, whoever he was,
   of whatever country,
      he might have been my brother,
         were the world different.

I think
    he would not have been lying there
        were the world different.
            I think

if I had known him,
    on his birthday,
        I would have made for him
           a great celebration.

In the Pasture

On the first day of snow, when the white curtain of winter
    began to stream down,
the house where I lived grew distant
    and at first it seemed imperative to hurry home.
But later, not much later, I began to see
    that soft snowbound house as I would always remember it,
and I would linger a long time in the pasture,
    turning in circles, staring
at all the crisp, exciting, snow-filled roads
    that led away.

Both Worlds

Forever busy, it seems,
  with words,
   finally
    I put the pen down

and crumple
  most of the sheets
   and leave one or two,
    sometimes a few,

for the next morning.
  Day after day—
   year after year—
    it has gone on this way,

I rise from the chair,
  I put on my jacket
   and leave the house
    for that other world—

the first one,
  the holy one—
   where the trees say
    nothing the toad says

nothing the dirt
  says nothing and yet
   what has always happened
    keeps happening:

the trees flourish,
　the toad leaps,
　　and out of the silent dirt
　　　the blood-red roses rise.

We Should Be Well Prepared

The way the plovers cry goodbye.
The way the dead fox keeps on looking down the hill
    with open eye.
The way the leaves fall, and then there's the long wait.
The way someone says: we must never meet again.
The way mold spots the cake,
the way sourness overtakes the cream.
The way the river water rushes by, never to return.
The way the days go by, never to return.
The way somebody comes back, but only in a dream.

Desire

So long as I am hanging on
I want to be young and noble.
I want to be bold.

So said the great buck, named Swirler,
as he stepped like a king past me
the week before he was arrow-killed.

And so said the wren in the bush
after another hard year
of love, of nest-life, of singing.

And so say I
every morning, just before sunrise,
wading the edge of the dark ocean.

I Ask Percy How I Should Live My Life (Ten)

Love, love, love, says Percy.
And run as fast as you can
along the shining beach, or the rubble, or the dust.

Then, go to sleep.
Give up your body heat, your beating heart.
Then, trust.

Swimming, One Day in August

It is time now, I said,
for the deepening and quieting of the spirit
among the flux of happenings.

Something had pestered me so much
I thought my heart would break.
I mean, the mechanical part.

I went down in the afternoon
to the sea
which held me, until I grew easy.

About tomorrow, who knows anything.
Except that it will be time, again,
for the deepening and quieting of the spirit.

Mornings at Blackwater

For years, every morning, I drank
from Blackwater Pond.
It was flavored with oak leaves and also, no doubt,
the feet of ducks.

And always it assuaged me
from the dry bowl of the very far past.

What I want to say is
that the past is the past,
and the present is what your life is,
and you are capable
of choosing what that will be,
darling citizen.

So come to the pond,
or the river of your imagination,
or the harbor of your longing,

and put your lips to the world.
And live
your life.

Who Said This?

Something whispered something
that was not even a word.
It was more like a silence
that was understandable.
I was standing
at the edge of the pond.
Nothing living, what we call living,
was in sight.
And yet, the voice entered me,
my body-life,
with so much happiness.
And there was nothing there
but the water, the sky, the grass.

This Day, and Probably Tomorrow Also

Full of thought, regret, hope dashed or not dashed yet,
full of memory, pride, and more than enough
of spilled, personal grief,

I begin another page, another poem.

So many notions fill the day! I give them
gowns of words, sometimes I give them
little shoes that rhyme.

What an elite life!

While somewhere someone is kissing a face that is crying.
While somewhere women are walking out, at two in the morning—
    many miles to find water.
While somewhere a bomb is getting ready to explode.

Of Goodness

How good
that the clouds travel, as they do,
like the long dresses of the angels
of our imagination,

or gather in storm masses, then break
with their gifts of replenishment,
and how good
that the trees shelter the patient birds

in their thick leaves,
and how good that in the field
the next morning
red bird frolics again, his throat full of song,

and how good
that the dark ponds, refreshed,
are holding the white cups of the lilies
so that each is an eye that can look upward,

and how good that the little blue-winged teal
comes paddling among them, as cheerful as ever,

and so on, and so on.

Meadowlark Sings and I Greet Him in Return

Meadowlark, when you sing it's as if
you lay your yellow breast upon mine and say
hello, hello, and are we not
of one family, in our delight of life?
You sing, I listen.
Both are necessary
if the world is to continue going around
night-heavy then light-laden, though not
everyone knows this or at least
not yet,

or, perhaps, has forgotten it
in the torn fields,

in the terrible debris of progress.

When I Cried for Help

Where are you, Angel of Mercy?
Outside in the dusk, among the flowers?
Leaning against the window or the door?
Or waiting, half asleep, in the spare room?

I'm here, said the Angel of Mercy.
I'm everywhere—in the garden, in the house,
and everywhere else on earth—so much
asking, so much to do. Hurry! I need you.

In the Evening, in the Pinewoods

Who knows the sorrows of the heart?
God, of course, and the private self.
But who else? Anyone or anything else?
Not the trees, in their windy independence.
Nor the roving clouds, nor, even, the dearest of friends.

Yet maybe the thrush, who sings
by himself, at the edge of the green woods,
to each of us
out of his mortal body, his own feathered limits,
of every estrangement, exile, rejection—their
   death-dealing weight.

And then, so sweetly, of every goodness also to be remembered.

Love Sorrow

Love sorrow. She is yours now, and you must
take care of what has been
given. Brush her hair, help her
into her little coat, hold her hand,
especially when crossing a street. For, think,

what if you should lose her? Then you would be
sorrow yourself; her drawn face, her sleeplessness
would be yours. Take care, touch
her forehead that she feel herself not so

utterly alone. And smile, that she does not
altogether forget the world before the lesson.
Have patience in abundance. And do not
ever lie or ever leave her even for a moment

by herself, which is to say, possibly, again,
abandoned. She is strange, mute, difficult,
sometimes unmanageable but, remember, she is a child.
And amazing things can happen. And you may see,

as the two of you go
walking together in the morning light, how
little by little she relaxes; she looks about her;
she begins to grow.

Of Love

I have been in love more times than one,
thank the Lord. Sometimes it was lasting
whether active or not. Sometimes
it was all but ephemeral, maybe only
an afternoon, but not less real for that.
They stay in my mind, these beautiful people,
or anyway people beautiful to me, of which
there are so many. You, and you, and you,
whom I had the fortune to meet, or maybe
missed. Love, love, love, it was the
core of my life, from which, of course, comes
the word for the heart. And, oh, have I mentioned
that some of them were men and some were women
and some—now carry my revelation with you—
were trees. Or places. Or music flying above
the names of their makers. Or clouds, or the sun
which was the first, and the best, the most
loyal for certain, who looked so faithfully into
my eyes, every morning. So I imagine
such love of the world—its fervency, its shining, its
innocence and hunger to give of itself—I imagine
this is how it began.

Eleven Versions of the Same Poem:

Am I lost?

Am I lost?
  I don't think so.

Do I know where I am?
  I'm not sure.

Have I ever been happier in my life?
  Never.

Am I lost?
  I am lost.

Do I know where I am?
  I am lost.

Have I ever been more joyful in my life?
  I am lost.

I don't want to live a small life

I don't want to live a small life. Open your eyes,
open your hands. I have just come
from the berry fields, the sun

kissing me with its golden mouth all the way
(open your hands) and the wind-winged clouds
following along thinking perhaps I might

feed them, but no I carry these heart-shapes
only to you. Look how many how small
but so sweet and maybe the last gift

I will ever bring to anyone in this
world of hope and risk, so do.
Look at me. Open your life, open your hands.

I am the one

I am the one
who took your hand
when you offered it to me.

I am the pledge of emptiness
that turned around.
Even the trees smiled.

Always I was the bird
that flew off through the branches.
Now

I am the cat
with feathers
under its tongue.

Now comes the long blue cold

Now comes the long blue cold
and what shall I say but that some
bird in the tree of my heart
is singing.

That same heart that only yesterday
was a room shut tight, without dreams.

Isn't it wonderful—the cold wind and
spring in the heart inexplicable.
Darling girl. Picklock.

So every day

So every day
I was surrounded by the beautiful crying forth
of the ideas of God,

one of which was you.

If the philosopher is right

If the philosopher is right,
that all we are
and all the earth around us
is only a dream,

even if a bright, long dream—
that everything is nothing
but what sits in the mind,

that the trees, that the red bird
are all in the mind,
and the river, and the sea in storm
are all in the mind,

that nothing exists fierce or soft or apt to be
    truly shaken—
nothing tense, wild, sleepy—nothing
like Yeats' girl with the yellow hair—
then you too are a dream

which last night and the night before that
    and the years before that
you were not.

There you were, and it was like spring

There you were, and it was like spring—
like the first fair water with the light on it,
    hitting the eyes.
Why are we made the way we are made, that to love
    is to want?
Well, you are gone now, and this morning I have walked out
    to the back shore,
to the ocean which, even if we think we have measured it,
    has no final measure.
Sometimes you can see the great whales there,
    breaching and playing.
Sometimes the swans linger just long enough
    for us to be astonished.
Then they lift their wings, they become again
    a part of the untouchable clouds.

Where are you?

Where are you?
Do you know that the heart has a dungeon?
Bring light! Bring light!

I wish I loved no one

I wish I loved no one,
I said, one long day.

You are a fool then,
said the old cripple
from the poorhouse.

You are a fool then,
said the young woman
tramping the road
with nothing, nothing.

I wish I loved no one,
I said on yet another long day.

You are a fool then,
said a wrinkled face
at the boarding house.
And she laughed.
A pitiful fool!

I will try

I will try.
I will step from the house to see what I see
and hear and I will praise it.
I did not come into this world
to be comforted.
I came, like red bird, to sing.
But I'm not red bird, with his head-mop of flame
and the red triangle of his mouth
full of tongue and whistles,
but a woman whose love has vanished,
who thinks now, too much, of roots
and the dark places
where everything is simply holding on.
But this too, I believe, is a place
where God is keeping watch
until we rise, and step forth again and—
but wait. Be still. Listen!
Is it red bird? Or something
inside myself, singing?

What is the greatest gift?

What is the greatest gift?
Could it be the world itself—the oceans, the meadowlark,
   the patience of the trees in the wind?
Could it be love, with its sweet clamor of passion?

Something else—something else entirely
   holds me in thrall.
That you have a life that I wonder about
   more than I wonder about my own.
That you have a life—courteous, intelligent—
   that I wonder about more than I wonder about my own.
That you have a soul—your own, no one else's—
   that I wonder about more than I wonder about my own.
So that I find my soul clapping its hands for yours
   more than my own.

Someday

Even the oldest of the trees continues its wonderful labor.
Hummingbird lives in one of them.
He's there for the white blossoms, and the secrecy.
The blossoms could be snow, with a dash of pink.
At first the fruit is small and green and hard.
Everything has dreams, hope, ambition.

If I could I would always live in such shining obedience
where nothing but the wind trims the boughs.
I am sorry for every mistake I have made in my life.
I'm sorry I wasn't wiser sooner.
I'm sorry I ever spoke of myself as lonely.

Oh, love, lay your hands upon me again.
Some of the fruit ripens and is picked and is delicious.
Some of it falls and the ants are delighted.
Some of it hides under the snow and the famished deer are saved.

Red Bird Explains Himself

"Yes, I was the brilliance floating over the snow
and I was the song in the summer leaves, but this was
only the first trick
I had hold of among my other mythologies,
for I also knew obedience: bringing sticks to the nest,
food to the young, kisses to my bride.

But don't stop there, stay with me: listen.

If I was the song that entered your heart
then I was the music of your heart, that you wanted and needed,
and thus wilderness bloomed there, with all its
followers: gardeners, lovers, people who weep
for the death of rivers.

And this was my true task, to be the
music of the body. Do you understand? for truly the body needs
a song, a spirit, a soul. And no less, to make this work,
the soul has need of a body,
and I am both of the earth and I am of the inexplicable
beauty of heaven
where I fly so easily, so welcome, yes,
and this is why I have been sent, to teach this to your heart."

I thank the editors of the following magazines in
which some of the poems have previously appeared,
sometimes in slightly different form.

Appalachia: "From This River, When I Was a Child,
    I Used to Drink"
Bark: "Percy (Nine)"
Cape Cod Voice: "Luke," "A River Far Away and Long Ago,"
    "There You Were, and It Was Like Spring"
Five Points: "Visiting the Graveyard," "Night Herons,"
    "Red"
Onearth: "Straight Talk from Fox," "Winter and the
    Nuthatch," "Showing the Birds"
Orion: "Boundaries"
Parabola: "There Is a Place Beyond Ambition," "Not This, Not That"
Portland Magazine: "This Day, and Probably Tomorrow Also,"
    "Of Goodness"
Reflections (Yale Divinity School): "The Teachers,"
    "Watching a Documentary about Polar Bears Trying to
    Survive on the Melting Ice Floes"
Shenandoah: "Red Bird"
The Southern Review: "With the Blackest of Inks,"
    "Invitation," "The Orchard," "In the Evening, in the
    Pinewoods"
Spiritus: "Night and the River"